cross stitch

# THE LORD IS MY SHEPHERD

BY HOLLY DeFOUNT

KOOLER DESIGN STUDIO



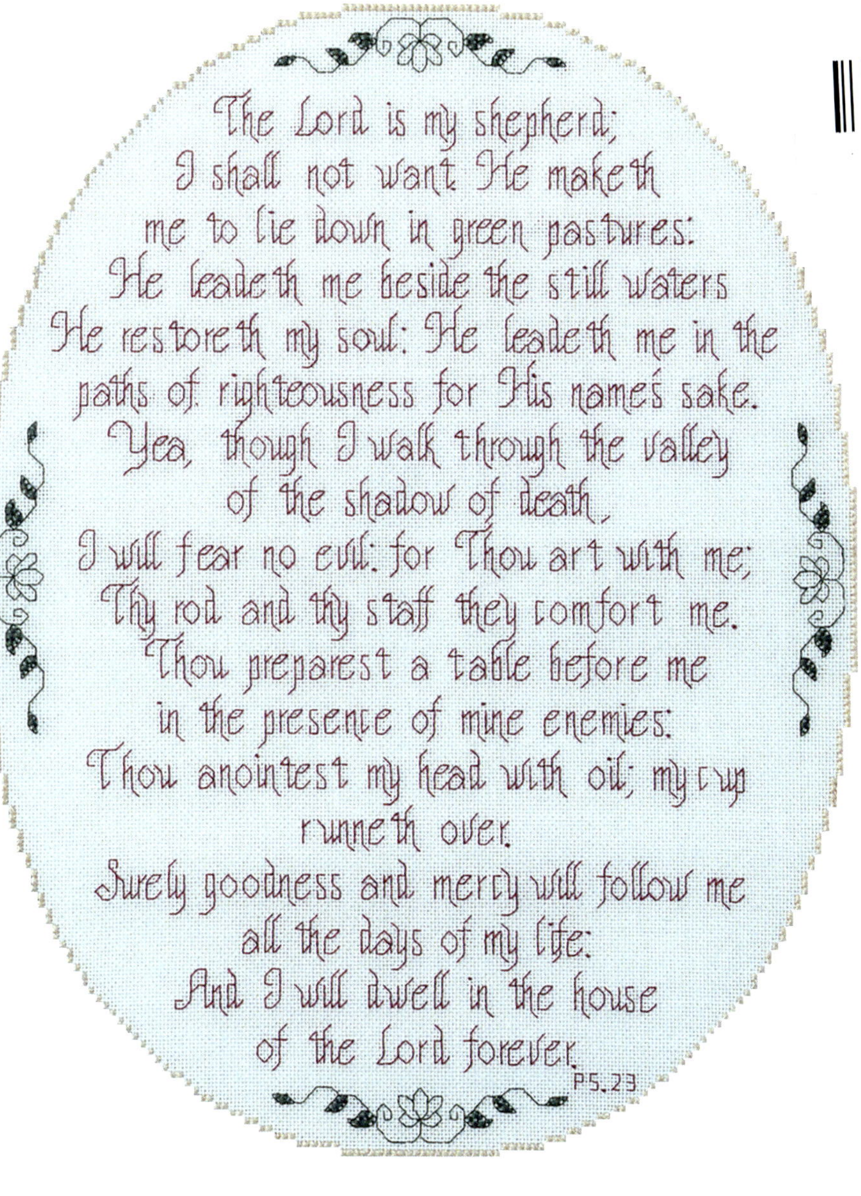


LEISURE ARTS INC • MAUMELLE, ARKANSAS

The Lord is my shepherd;
I shall not want. He maketh
me to lie down in green pastures:
He leadeth me beside the still waters.
He restoreth my soul: He leadeth me in the
paths of righteousness for His names sake.
Yea, though I walk through the valley
of the shadow of death,
I will fear no evil: for thou art with me;
thy rod and thy staff they comfort me.
Thou preparest a table before me
in the presence of mine enemies:
Thou anointest my head with oil; my cup

**THE LORD IS MY SHEPHERD (120w x 178h)**

| X | DMC | 1/4X | B'ST | ANC. | COLOR |
|---|---|---|---|---|---|
| | blanc | | | 2 | white |
| | 319 | | | 218 | green |
| | 367 | | | 217 | lt green |
| | 415 | | | 398 | grey |
| | 738 | | | 361 | tan |
| | 797 | | | 132 | vy dk blue |
| | 798 | | | 131 | dk blue |
| | 799 | | | 136 | blue |
| | 800 | | | 144 | vy lt blue |
| | 809 | | | 130 | lt blue |
| | 839 | | | 360 | dk brown |
| | 840 | | | 379 | brown |
| | 841 | | | 378 | lt brown |
| | 3345 | | | 268 | dk yellow green |
| | 3346 | | | 267 | yellow green |
| | 3347 | | | 266 | lt yellow green |
| | 3685 | | | 1028 | mauve |
| | 3799 | | | 236 | dk grey |
| | 3685 | | | 1028 | mauve Fr. Knot |

Grey area indicates first row of bottom section of design.

# GENERAL INSTRUCTIONS

## WORKING WITH CHART

**How To Read Chart:** The design is shown in chart form. Each colored square on the chart represents one Cross Stitch. Each colored triangle on the chart represents one Quarter Stitch. Colored dots represent French Knots. The straight lines on the chart indicate Backstitch. When a Backstitch crosses a square, the symbol is omitted.

The chart is accompanied by a color key. This key indicates the color of floss to use for each stitch on the chart. The headings on the color key are for Cross Stitch **(X)**, DMC color number **(DMC)**, Quarter Stitch **(1/4 X)**, Backstitch **(B'ST)**, Anchor color number **(ANC.)**, and color name **(COLOR)**. Color key columns should be read vertically and horizontally to determine type of stitch and floss color.

## STITCHING TIP

**Working Over Two Fabric Threads:** Use the sewing method instead of the stab method when working over two fabric threads. To use the sewing method, keep your stitching hand on the right side of the fabric (instead of stabbing the fabric with the needle and taking your stitching hand to the back of the fabric to pick up the needle). With the sewing method, you take the needle down and up with one stroke instead of two. To add support to stitches, it is important that the first Cross Stitch is placed on the fabric with stitch 1-2 beginning and ending where a vertical fabric thread crosses over a horizontal fabric thread ***(Fig. 1)***. When the first stitch is in the correct position, the entire design will be placed properly, with vertical fabric threads supporting each stitch.

**Fig. 1**

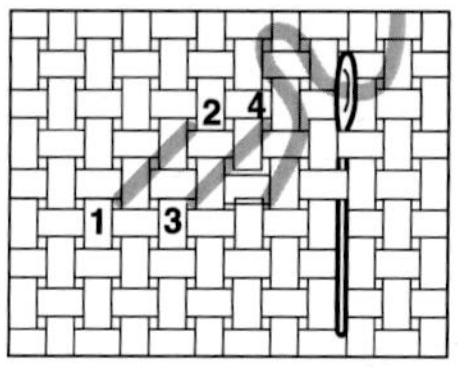

## STITCH DIAGRAMS

**Counted Cross Stitch (X):** Work one Cross Stitch to correspond to each colored square on the chart. For horizontal rows, work stitches in two journeys ***(Fig. 2)***. For vertical rows, complete each stitch as shown ***(Fig. 3)***. When working over two fabric threads, work Cross Stitch as shown in **Fig. 4**. When the chart shows a Backstitch crossing a colored square ***(Fig. 5)***, a Cross Stitch ***(Fig. 2, 3, or 4)*** should be worked first; then the Backstitch ***(Fig. 8 or 9)*** should be worked on top of the Cross Stitch.

**Fig. 2**

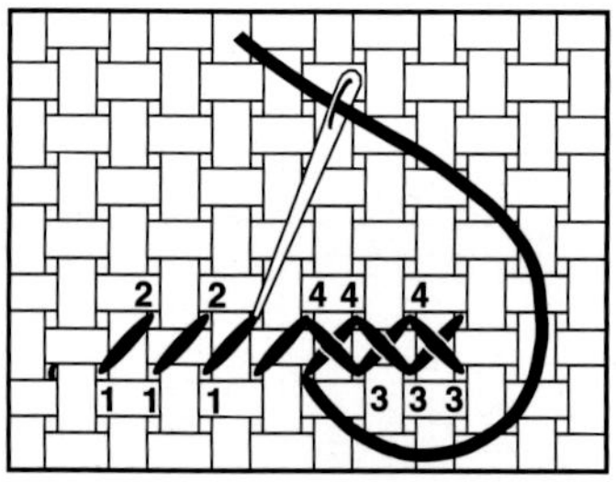

**Fig. 3**

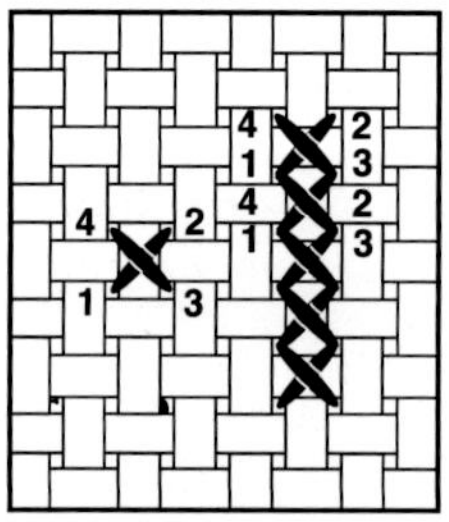

**Fig. 4**

**Fig. 5**

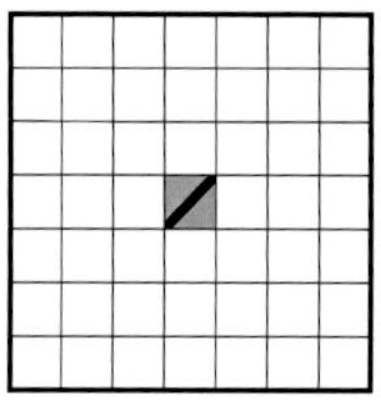

**Quarter Stitch (1/4 X):** Quarter Stitches are denoted by triangular shapes of color on the chart and on the color key. Come up at 1 ***(Fig. 6)***; then split fabric thread to go down at 2. **Fig. 7** shows the technique for Quarter Stitch when working over two fabric threads.

**Fig. 6**

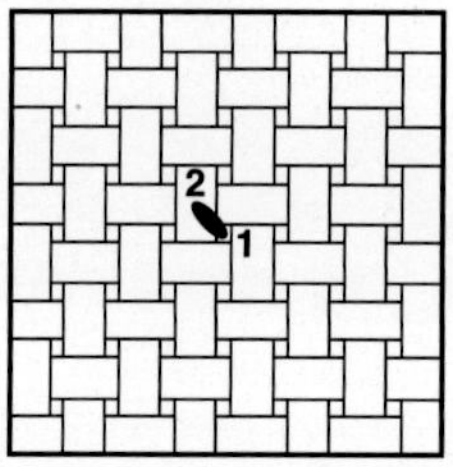

**Fig. 7**

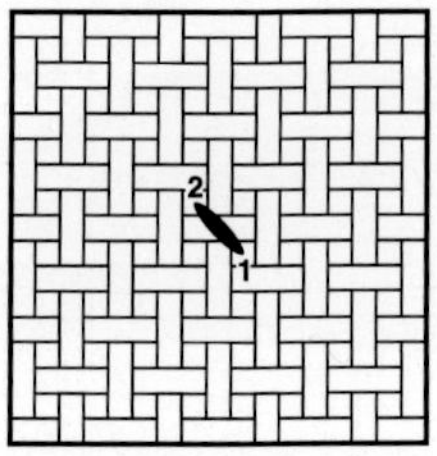

**Backstitch (B'ST):** For outline detail, Backstitch (shown on chart and on color key by colored straight lines) should be worked after the design has been completed ***(Fig. 8)***. When working over two fabric threads, work Backstitch as shown in **Fig. 9**.

**Fig. 8**

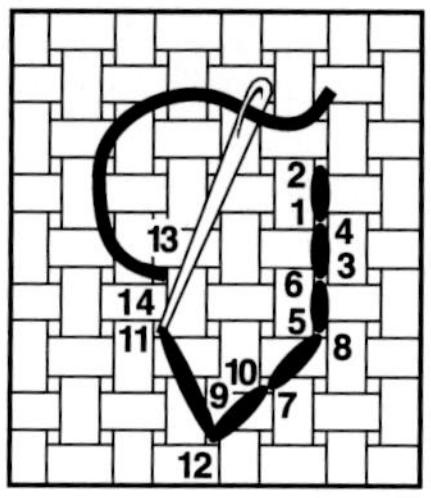

**Fig. 9**

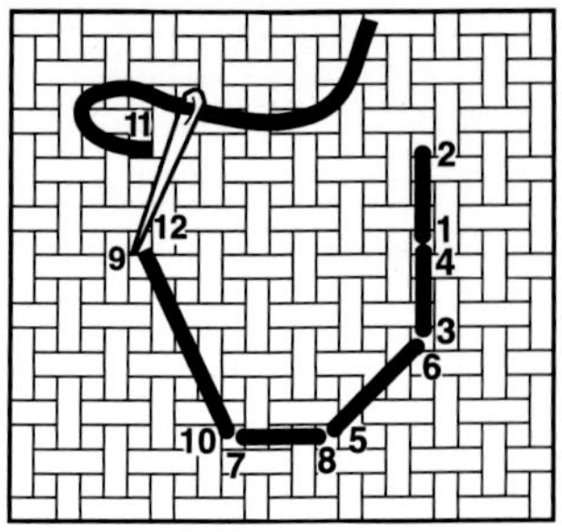

**French Knot:** Bring needle up at 1. Wrap floss once around needle and insert needle at 2, holding end of floss with non-stitching fingers ***(Fig. 10)***. Tighten knot; then pull needle through fabric, holding floss until it must be released. For larger knot, use more strands; wrap only once.

**Fig. 10**

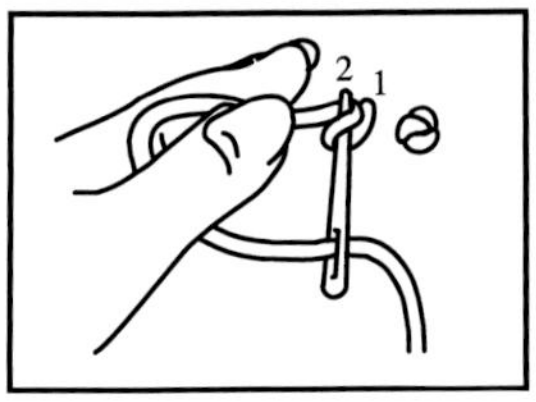

# PROJECT

**The Lord Is My Shepherd** — Antique White Lugana (25 ct) — stitched over two fabric threads using 3 strands of floss for Cross Stitch and 1 strand for Backstitch and French Knots — approx design size 9 5/8" x 14 1/4" — custom framed.



Made in U.S.A.